Getting Through It

The Literature of Missing Persons
previous titles from Geoff Peterson

Cordes Junction (1887)
Medicine Dog (novel, 1989)
Hecho en Mexico (chapbook, 1995)
Bad Trades (novel, 2000)
Cold Reading (2007)
Crazy Stairs (2008)
Drama & Desire (2009)
The Greyhound Bardo (novel, 2009)
Cine Bahía: The Suicide Codex (2009)
Fiery Messengers (2010)
She Dropped Me in the Middle of Nowhere (2011)
Dark is my Therapy (2011)
Tucumcari (with Megan Collins, 2012)
The Perry Square Gospels (2012)
Penance (2013)
punto: poems with time running out (2013)
Horrible Intimacies (2014)
The Moira Cycle (2015)
Not Sleep, Deeper: on aging & living alone (2016)
No Services: 69 haiku for your driving pleasure (2917)
The Folding Chairs Meditation: prompts for a season on the skids (2017)
3:30: *nocturnes & études* (2017)
Trance States: memory, apparitions, and the movies in my gut (2018)
Archipelago: selected early poems (2019)
Death Work: the late poems (2019)
Alone, with groceries: notes on a passing world (2020)
Breakfast for Dinner: poems over easy (2020)
Open Ticket: postmortem sketches (2021)

In the Underground Garage: poems incognito (2021)
5 O 'clock Shadow (stories, 2021)
False-Positive: The Quarantine Verses (2022)
The Directions to Blue Willow: out-takes & repairs (2023)
The Book of Leaving: notes, drafts & extracts (2024)
The Dips (with art by Sharon Butler, 2024)

*Titles available at amazon.com, barnes&noble.com,
or through your local bookseller.*

Getting Through It
poems by geoff peterson

Gotham Books

30 N Gould St.
Ste. 20820, Sheridan, WY 82801
https://gothambooksinc.com/

Phone: 1 (307) 464-7800

© 2024 *Geoff Peterson*. All rights reserved.

No part of this book may be reproduced, stored in a retrieval system, or transmitted by any means without the written permission of the author.

Published by Gotham Books (December 28, 2024)

ISBN: 979-8-3306-2907-7 (P)
ISBN: 979-8-3306-2908-4 (E)

Because of the dynamic nature of the Internet, any web addresses or links contained in this book may have changed since publication and may no longer be valid.

The views expressed in this work are solely those of the author and do not necessarily reflect the views of the publisher, and the publisher hereby disclaims any responsibility for them.

for Joshua Hurand,
counselor, poet, friend,
rest in peace.

Does one take flowers along to the land of the dead?
Flowers are only lent to us, the truth is that we go.
We leave flowers and songs and the earth.
The truth is that we go.
—Aztec poet
Jacques Soustelle, trans.

Getting to It
(by way of introduction)

Every book, if it's honest, deals with the same theme: *the decision in choosing life or death.*

That's my unvarnished opinion.

Today, for example…
I cooked a pretty good plate of shrimp and Brussels sprouts spooned over rice, but being absent of feeling in my good hand, dropped it en route to the table—and it splattered.

Being too diffuse to clean up—at least in one helping, (and besides, it's all the food there was) you do what you must: *Please be seated on the floor and with both hands eat it up, eat it all up—like a good boy.*

In that moment, since writing makes it so, I became my mother, slumped over, hopeless…staring at the mess like it were raw sewage, and began to be miserable. Any second her sobs would burst forth and wild rice fly from her lips.

Life is sweet, they say, but there are no happy endings in this world, or why would we care? Suffering may be postponed but not avoided. No happy endings, and everything happens for the last time.

geoff p.
2024

The List

Getting to It (Introduction) viii
Farewell Tour 1
Luna Park 2
The Hummingbird Patois 3
Afternoon Shower 4
Book of Songs 5
Desierto 6
Mirage 7
Phone Call, Late 8
Bus to Nogales 9
Life Story 10
The Main Event 11
The Wisdom of the Desert 12
My Last Mission 13
Roadside Assistance 14
Más Qué Nada 15
Black Hole 16
The Cost of It 17
Stanislav 18
Café du Nord 19
In Repose 20
Dental Appointment 21
Past Midnight 22
Last of His Tribe 23
Dawn Patrol 24
Conspiracy Theory 25
Love Song, A7 26
Covid Days 27
Heat Advisory 28
Breakfast at Noon 29
Meditation 30
Disgust 31

Prize Worthy	32
Pain Management	34
1000 appointments	35
Waiting to Fly	36
Big Hand, Little Hand	37
Pulmonary Function	39
To the Fire Ant by the Pool	40
The Mileage	41
Changing Chairs	42
And Now This	43
Energy	44
Bad News	45
The Flight Out	46
It was a calm and moonlit sea…	47
Noise	48
Wisp	49
Turbulence	50
Itinerary	51
Testament	52
First Light	53
A Year Doing Nothing	54
Tao, a handbook	55
Poems Like Us	56
Night Prayers	57
Siren Call	58
Out-of-Body	59
Walt Whitman Takes the Greyhound	60
Late Call	61
Travels with Charley	62
The End	63
Vermeer	64
Days Without Grace	65
Missing Person 46	66
Exerunt	67

Dear Diary 68
Getting Through It 70
At My Desk 71
2 Men the Same Age 72
Laces 73
What He's Capable of 74
At Reagan International 76
Flight Manifest 77
Killing Time Between 78
The Silence 79
The Famine 80
Hummingbird Press 81
At Rest 82
My Last Chance 83
You Will See the Ocean Before Dying 84
The Last Reading 85

I Acknowledge… 86
About the Author: 88

Farewell Tour

I should've driven instead.
I'd have left at dusk and cruised all night on a tank of gas,
then got a room the next day to avoid
holiday traffic.

Can't sleep, can't stay awake, I'd gas up singing the blues
from Chicago and drive the next day commiserating
with ghosts and goblins on the Lincoln Highway,
while the night hums and rolls over pasture.

But I flew instead as someone bought the ticket
when they said I shouldn't drive alone.
Not ready for this—*clear for take-off…*
God help me get this in the air.

Napkins with coffee at airport counters
say *No one wants to die—get flight insurance
or be sorry.*

Luna Park

How wonderful to roam familiar trails without care, fresh out
of what to call things.

Walking past an abandoned ball field when a bruised hardball
lands with a thud:

home run, a walk-off to the raggedy cheers of families
a thousand innings ago—comes now with urgency
when life stops being a surprise and becomes a medium.

This meteor decided whether to strike me dead or land
close enough to startle.

It must've known where life was headed,
while at the same time hauling from deep space
our thunderous applause.

The Hummingbird Patois

Seizures begin with not engaging the body, but
ahead of yourself in two places at once,
says a neurologist.

Selfish with my time, I keep appointments to please,
and come out chirping a hummingbird patois
like I'm paid up for a while.

Of course it's come to this.

Afternoon Shower

A few drops splashed upon the windshield:
a cat's paw scamper.

A wind, a cloud stooping to shake out her hair…
I am old enough to be a child again.

Desert hills shimmer as under water,
a broken-winged blackbird's sputter at dusk.

Wind gusts and sun spots convene to soothe
a nervous heart's panic.

Book of Songs

Taking a leak at Omar's GasUp, relaxed…
when something huge from the fan brushes my cheek—
a cockroach or a bat catching a ride to Sonoyta.
But today he'll end up drowning in a gold cloud
when flushed in a rusty gulp at the bottom.

It's okay—somehow, some way he'll make the passage
whirling through circuits of underground pipes
beneath the international border…

and end upright in the plaza, reciting poems in Spanish.

Desierto

Sonoita...Patagonia...Sierra Vista...
run your eyes over the names like reading a menu...
Bonita...Sahuarita... Now chew the vowels
like leaves of a rare medicinal plant
courtesy of the dead.

Mirage

Suck it up, old man.
Let the heat beat down and cicadas whine
like ammo belts of desire going off in the trees.

No woman, no juice, and tuckered from thinking,
no love story the kind you sought in vain…
Bear it, the burden of yourself to the next oasis.

Phone Call, Late

Don't ask why it's important
but I want you to know my frustration with my life
and the urgency to get it done.

It's not about the money
but about closure and completing the last official task
before dying.

Got it, I said, and did not mean to question her decision
to wrangle with her dead partner's bank. In fact,
I'd dare go the 10 rounds myself, except it
would've been for the money.

You make me laugh, she said.

Bus to Nogales

Mostly old couples bound for the border
with prescriptions for cheap medicine or a date
with a dentist.

Borrowed from a branch library, a fat
memoir of someone you'd know from before.
Nothing so tedious as a man's adulterous affair
running to a thousand pages…

While seated at the window
a college sophomore rides with her *tía*,
a shrunken woman preaching caution in savage times,
and insists on getting lunch on the Mexico side.

   Next stop,
Rio Rico, says the driver.
By then I'd quit reading and got off alone
for the slim chance of rain.

Life Story

What a man yearns to tell a woman named Lana at check-out:
his origin, struggle, and close calls…

That's when you know it's useless,
when you can't bear to tell the old saga again—
when a life loses its flavor.

Now where were we? In bed, yes, a lover,
your first night, the next day's news yet unread in the papers,
in which everyone who died is watching.

The Main Event

Every doctor who takes money
prescribes exercises to keep me alive:
stretches with bands lashed to door knobs,
purposeful walks at dawn,
or lying on the floor, feet up
and lifting 15 lb. weights…
Hand stretches for carpal tunnel,
one with putty—with or without brace.
Others that make shadow figures
on the ceiling like nights with sweats
and you pray for death.
There's more but I won't go into it,
except to say: with so much time
sweating an extra few reps,
you have to ask yourself—
for what?

The Wisdom of the Desert

Sayings of the 4th century desert fathers in translation
by Thomas Merton...

Already I'd sensed the end when I hitched to the Salton Sea
and pitched a tent, too nervous about snakes to sleep in the open.
Maybe I knew by the end I was fading, walking dead,
as it were, but that it would take time.

How could I know—fifty years on I'd blow dust off its cover
and blush to read what I'd scribbled there.
Lord have mercy—meaning, I suppose,
a plea to outlive my strangeness.

My Last Mission

Alone as much as I'd always desired
but couldn't admit—to you, or her, or the one called myself…
Those who wore solitude as a badge of honor—young and lunatic.
I listen to them on short-wave crackling between broadcasts,
but fail to recognize myself speaking…
mayday, are you there? Come in—
while a life bursts with static.

Once a Japanese regular, I panicked
and deserted my unit in the battle's last fury,
and lay underground with the dead
and the oily worms…

On the sixth day I crawled out
and climbed the hill most fought over,
then saw the wakes of a thousand ships
glistening on the horizon.

Alone I wandered, wind battered, starving,
abandoned on an unmanned island in a lost ravine,
while the one who would become my father
sailed west to the next campaign.

Roadside Assistance

We met one night at a point in the journey
anything can happen. Carl and I stopped
to help the girl in shorts change a tire.
Headed north, she said, to meet friends
who waited to have fun.

Next we met up at a truck stop in Oregon
or was it Idaho, and smoked up her cigarettes.
When time came to go she gave me a book
and wrote inside it's okay if I'd ever think to call
from no place in particular.

"No pressure," she winked.

I walked to her car, leaned in and remarked
how bold was her candor… "Can do," she joked,
flashing a high sign like she'd just stepped from a poster
aimed to rally the home front.

She drove off and I woke up on a transport
bound for Australia. Never would it happen, I thought,
being old and she fresh out of college.

Más Qué Nada

Write it because at least it's something.
Maybe better to just relax with that
and let it sink in:

*Nothing is nothing other
than what came before.*
The great ones knew it
and you should too,
so write it.

Wade into it until you're hardly here.
And don't move or the light will collapse
like bones breaking…

and *poof*—everything!

Destiny as written is having something to say,
when something else comes out
instead.

Black Hole

"I'm suffocating," she cried,
daughter of darkness and powerful delusions.

Now after twelve years learning to live since
she vacated the premises: a hole
where my life had been.

Today I am here hardly dressed and attending
to one thing at a time.

On good days it works; otherwise,
nothing but photos I cannot tell apart from the sky.
Still I persist while the hollow hours burst.

The Cost of It

A deep seeded anger toward the Other—
call it God then—it surfaces during
periods of stress and my nerves
unsheathed. Call it a matter
of loyalty to the mother,
an impatience with things
that once gave pleasure:
music, sex, public places…
It feeds an unease
at the base of the spine
that a man runs from always.
So with your permission
I'll put my breakdown right out there,
on record, and let the chips fall…
The author will now sign copies
of his latest in the lobby.
Thank you for coming,
and drive safely.

Stanislav

A man must weep each day to get through it.
Wounds exist so deep they heal
only if the dead are met.

Therapy in the ancient sense
means treating the soul for lesions.
A man rises and sinks in prolonged bouts
of confusion.

He wearies, you see, the man grows weary
of everything he thought was for keeps.
Nothing is for keeps.

Meditate, my friend, weep prodigiously,
and walk away when it's time.
Now go. Call me when you
forget who you are.

Café du Nord

France again. Not the one you know
from before, but the gray wet coast of men and nets
from which the tourists have all gone home.

Here the woman alone at the table chooses the man,
and only has to disguise it to let him know it all
starts with him.

Thin, narrow-hipped, freckled with hair coming loose,
she allows it: a most delicate moment to witness…
especially if it's you she means to make
her next assignment.

In Repose

For a man living alone
there are moments he understands
who he is and why it had to be this way.
While dreaming he's found on his bed
in repose with the song of hummingbirds
sealed to his blue lips.
So much goes on
before we ever arrive
at the scene.

Dental Appointment

Michelle, I'm feeling light-headed today,
I fear you'll not find much plaque
to hack and hew at.

And she replies it's when we're most light-headed
that we're most delusional.

But I can't seem to keep my eyes open,
so how do I keep my mouth stretched wide?

X-rays, she says, for an extra hundred dollars.
Now bite down for me.

Her boss surveys my uppers and says
it will take two crowns and a bridge for starters.

They're suggesting I put four thousand dollars
into my mouth so I can go home and die.

Makes me laugh—even with a drill in my mouth.
The last time I was given laughing gas,
I was told never to come back.

Past Midnight

The peace it brings to watch my hobbled neighbor walking his dog…

reminds me how lovely is being alone.

Last of His Tribe

Of all those who came west in the last century
to see for themselves…

Grandpa the father's father, Jack the mother's,
Kitty, Ward, Jacqueline, the cousins…

Crazy Jimmy had once got as far as Detroit.
He's dead now. They all are.

Only one remains, the lost child,
an old man who releases the hours in the bent light.

Dawn Patrol

Calm, rested, in no hurry to bail or exaggerate to be heard,
he breathes from the belly to better assess
what's coming.

Sitting without hunger,
he will dive for days without moving,
recalling an old sub found at 3000'
beneath the surface, "sitting upright
and relatively intact,"
said the report.

Living alone, a man becomes fragile without
intimacy, and will be found slumped
in his chair with a book about
boats he'd hurried to catch.

Conspiracy Theory

My friend says
the man running for president
will be assassinated
and a real dictator
like we've not seen—
will take over.

You laugh, it's the truth!

My friend misunderstands.
I'm not laughing because I don't
believe what he says,
I laugh because I do.

Love Song, A7

Love me, goes the ballad—
A7 on the jukebox.
Play D3, no—F9, says the barmaid:
same words, same machine drumming,
any notion of melody dispensed with
for being too hard.

Love me, and please don't listen
to anything I say when I'm like this…
Before our names and our points of view,
you were nearer to me
than breath.

Play *that* tune.

Covid Days

Sorrow makes us beautiful while we bear it
into the next world.

Since the pandemic my friend suffers brain fog,
and forgets what it was she lost.

Some days she gets invited to funerals
for people she's never heard of.

Heat Advisory

On days like this I sit in the dark
with a fan and stare—at nothing really.
I stare and still it's barely enough.
Barely hanging on, I tell friends,
but I'm getting used to it,
bug-bitten in a bungalow
beside the tracks. That's
as real as I allow it
to ever get. You see,
on some nights
the light from
an oncoming train
appears out of
nowhere.

Breakfast at Noon

She looked middle-aged,
but was older than what's counted in years.

When I clasped her beneath each arm to lift
from her wheelchair, she grasped at
the air to better lean into it—
not a scrap of strength anywhere.

For an hour I'd watched her by the window,
and sensed she'd been alone
since birth and lived her body's tenure
disabled. I asked a waitress
was she in fact a regular,
but no one had seen her before,
nor most likely again.

Some people's lives a plea for help.
Was she not sent to remind me
we are not alone, and that
words ultimately fail?

Meditation

When you've said goodbye to the world we call home,
you find there's nowhere left to land,
and can rest easy.

An old man told me if I wished to return to the islands
of my father, to merely close my eyes and…
waves would begin to appear.

Disgust

In the dream I'm the guest of honor at a conference
where my poems hang in dolorous hallways,
and a student hired to make me accountable
hands me my mail—a piece at a time.
In all a dozen letters, postmarked
years before—from old loves
once disposed to flight.
Anything else, I ask,
looking up.
     No, she says,
except her father died and cut her
from the will in favor of an airline hostess
who entered his life at a sore point in transition.
I admit I'd once loved her myself
and it went as you'd expect—
the hostess, I mean.
When the kid left I lay for an hour,
and waited for tears to come
that just wouldn't.

Prize Worthy

I don't know what to say.
Before I would've crept inside you
and burst like an infection.
But it's too late for that,
you don't know me.

I saw your book on the Used shelf
in the back by the toilet,
and if I no longer buy books,
I bought yours, drove it home
and devoured one page then another.

A skinny book I'm not able to finish
if it means putting it down.

It won every prize worth noting
in the year it came out.
Barely a child, I'd wager.
Look at that picture:
serenity of mood found in both worlds.
So lovely, the part in your hair,
the cheeks without makeup.

Since then, the grants followed
that allow one to move about:
Italy, Spain, Iceland…
without having to teach to make a living,
but free to work in their archives and
jot notes while walking.

How it strikes me like an arrow—the life
I might've lived, being awarded.
Makes me swoon to think about it.
No wonder the women left,
they knew, you see,
what I'd become,
spending my little money
to land and sleep on friends' floors,
and give my books for free.

Pain Management

It's not like before
when asked to give pain a number,
but left where no one meets you
where you're at, as all the science
drops off, and what's left
are hours breathing, dozing off
and getting to the toilet.

One night the pain spikes
where the numbers shatter and
you can no longer be with yourself,
but will seek an exit by any means.
A doctor reports his one case
of a "10" so far: a musician
with cancer of the inner ear,
screaming to be sprung from her body.
Pain then, enough to drive a stake
and force an eruption.

I think of my mother
banging her head on the linoleum
to be let go of by God.
I think of my ex-wife, mother of
my children, hunched in a hayloft
on a cold night in January
with a revolver…

1000 appointments

My surefire defense against the allure of suicide:
meal planning,

when everything tastes like yesterday and
the day before…

Today I will no longer have what it takes
to answer the phone.

Wait, who's there? Barely a knock at the door.
Coming, I am coming!

Waiting to Fly

Life out here in a garden under the stars,
with a breeze after the heat's lifted…
I got to admit—not so bad.

Green glimmer of water in a pool
while the moon hangs tilted at ten o'clock…
It's just me now, after all these years,
talking to myself.

You never think it comes to this,
you think someone calls and invites you back
to before when the bed was enough
for both.

Or maybe an idea for kick-starting the heart
to open and admit you're hungry.
Am I hungry?

Tomorrow I'll take off and land somewhere,
then rent a room and consider the hours
being who I am.

Big Hand, Little Hand

I can't say why I make these appointments.
I suppose they're made for me as
one doctor refers me to another,
who refers me further along.
I jot it in a calendar to make sure I shave,
shower and find my keys in time.

They want an MRI of my brain
to see where the voices come from,
and to find what explains my poor
decisions in traffic.

Showing up is a big deal,
and blackouts are can be hazardous.
Today I was scheduled to see
my physical trainer, but had to scramble
after reading the clock wrong.

Big hand, little hand, I get them confused
or don't see enough when looking.
     Or perhaps
it's Freudian and I resist
the whole project
called coping.

Why have you come to see me, she inquires.
I tell her it's been years and I wish to catch up.
How have you been, Marian,
I see time has been kind—
that sort of thing.

She orders I close my eyes
and walk a straight line until I am told
to stop.
      There is much to weigh, she says,
in the commotion of a life before you can make
a reasonable decision.

Amen, sister.

Pulmonary Function

Appointment for 7 a.m.,
it's best you arrive early for check-in.
Enter through Emergency and take the main concourse
to the solarium where someone will meet you.
You are the first patient they will see today.
Neither of them has had their coffee,
so it's best you be ready.

Just straight ahead to that cubicle at the end.
You'll find a chair to set your things on
and a stool inside the booth.
Now insert this tube in your mouth
and breathe normal, can you
do that for me?

Okay, suck in hard…and hold: 5-4-3-
what's the matter? I told you: breathe normal.
Try it again. *Bree-athe*…now blow and…
stop. Suck in hard…
and hold!

Wait—we have a problem.
Nurse, could you come in here?
I think there's a problem.

To the Fire Ant by the Pool

How goes it, my squiggly friend,
and how's your load today,
scrambling on all fours like
a ricocheted bullet.
Everybody's looking for something:
a piece of food, piece of ass,
a piece of the good life…
assurances that all will be well.
Listen, I'd love to stay and talk,
but I've got laps to swim
before my lungs blow out
and my heart goes up
in a 4-alarm blaze.

The Mileage

A mile, considered:
the number of steps from home to school,
from school to her house—whatever it takes.
The distance from the car trudging through drifts
for gas or food or a phone call to before…
The trail through waves of heat
to get to a house without purpose,
but that the miles may stop
and melt away.

Changing Chairs

In his office on Wednesdays I came reporting same:
tedium, rage, anxiety, visits from persons
missing from before while clocks tick
and nuclear dust settles.

Come, he said, change chairs with me
and say what you think I would say if the roles
were reversed.

So we did, and God, inside of minutes
I saw what I mourned and it wasn't the loss of M
from my last affair, but the M I'd lost
from the beginning!

When we finished I rose and stepped forth
feeling the space between myself and yesterday.
I was safe inside me.

Are you ready, he said. You don't have to go if
you're not ready.
I am, I said.

Now, are we ready? Tell me,
are you eager to do this? Switch now
and see where this goes and what it elicits
in the course of the poem.
Step boldly so that
anything might happen.

And Now This
(for Al Z.)

They stole my car, the gangs did.
Even to me it happens,
as listed on my report.

She wasn't much, a fractured fender
fastened with duct tape, and wobbly wheels
like a drunk on a treadmill.

But she'd start right up, easy on gas,
blessed with clear radio reception…
and she was all I had.

They strip her for parts, the gangs do,
then leave what's left on a remote backstreet
or parked in a girlfriend's garage.

Out of dozens in the lot, they chose mine
to cross the border and seek a target
in Zacatecas, I'll bet.

Hold it. Maybe it needed to happen so you'd have it
to write about. You know, chaos precedes
genius sort of thing.

Think of it as an opportunity! You're being asked
to walk in a straight line, eyes shut, until instructed to stop.

Stop right there.
Not another word.
Not today, thank you.

Energy

I must have to live,
and even tell myself I want to—
live I mean—and that
it's not just a matter of my brain
telling me things I decide to
unravel, but first there must be
energy in the blood
that tells the brain it's good
just being here, even if it—
no, especially if it takes
everything I've got.

Bad News

Back when trouble struck, or snakes came twitching,
it was okay as long as the car sat parked, gassed up.
You knew you could drive to a deserted place
and wait with renewed urgency.

But miles fade with age, and you fear being caught
with insufficient funds, an expired license.

Left alone to face it you'll make calls to insurance robots
who speak in tongues.

Even the world on nightly TV, you fail to recognize
ever having a place in.

You get calls from neighbors to help them climb stairs,
or drive them to the clinic.

And it terrifies to see where it's going,
that life as we know it bets against the house
till they put you in a room at the end of the hall
where the food is cold and roommates leave in bags.

I've seen that room when visiting others, and saw it for the rats,
and the ants, and cockroaches…

Are you sure you want to read further? There's still time.
You don't have to go through it, you could read
a weeper and marvel at how mild people were.
You could call them, you could leave a message.
You could say you forget why you called
but *tell me, how's it going?*

The Flight Out

Got my phone, my bag, passport & ticket…
a boarding pass that allows me to cross
a jet bridge to an incubator of unruly
standbys and the blood lust of others.
Now bid me safe passage and shut
the door—lock it and seal.
I promise not to look ahead.
I remember watching clouds
for previews of coming attractions.
But no more, I know what's coming next.
I know the drill of making the rounds
half choked in farewell.

It was a calm and moonlit sea…

Of course there's a woman in the form of a fish
or cliffs of carved radiance.
See how it comes in waves
and the moiling sea-foam of the shallows…
the kind of fate sealed and delivered
before time.

How long must one walk these shores without
coming face-to-face? There are no more
lights from the cities, nor from flights
to both coasts, nor the light from
boats looming in the channel.

I would finish the stubborn book I'd started,
then put on music—an old Fauré!—
scratchy after all these years…
and let it play, play,
until I'd lose my hearing
and I'd forget.

Noise

The world's in chaos,
as read from a teleprompter.
Newscasters slur their words,
and vomit comes out in tongues.

Litigants suing exes
while algorithms repair algorithms…
Jets fall from the sky, and we
pay bills we shouldn't have to.

Watch what happens to know
what they're selling.
Insurance, that's it—
just the ticket.

Wisp

The air creases and
zips up where a bat finds a pocket.
Zip, it's not there!
Swipe your hair to make sure,
and sense the space between
being and not being—is thin air!
So thin that—well, let's say
it's one and the same.
Bats/no bats: the blink of an eye.
Now we are speaking
of what death is.

Turbulence

Another good morning:
up early, sunlight purring softly over clean sheets…

I wake up convinced there's a flight to somewhere—
a.m. or p.m., it's booked.

Here I enter a cloud of turbulence
and radio maydays seeking instructions.
I've nothing to wear but wrinkled slacks in a suitcase.

Am I in the right place,
am I set at the right coordinates?
Am I doing what's meant to be done?

No matter what, you'll wander off course
and die alone tapping your chest in a desert shack.

I know why old folks load up on stuff—enough to last
till the end shows up. Does it show up?
    Ask yourself:
what have I missed being me,
who I am, or rather, not being me—
who that is.

Steady now, our pilot coaxes at cruising altitude
in a fairy-tale voice.

Itinerary

Some bleak scenes
a tourist cannot resist:
closing the eyes on approach
to a ghost lair to seek a floor's
creaking…nails and hinges
crumbling to the touch,
the mineral scent
from a played-out mine.

The half-lit motel that boasts
Cleaner Than Most
at the edge of the desert's
last gleaming.
Instead of refrigeration,
an ice chest and
appliances without plugs.

Home is exactly
the last place
headed for
and not found till later,
says the scrawl above the toilet.

Testament

Nobody else will do it,
so starting now I'll quote myself
from letters scattered among
the archipelagos…
and remind the others
of what's written in longhand
regarding matters of dire
personal consequence.
Words, you see, a burden
or nothing at all,
the last barrier reef
before infinity.

First Light

At my age,
to awaken is to
come from a long way off.
The sea, perhaps,
and islands yet distinguished
due to embargo and the
misreading of maps.
We know what is meant
without knowing and
travel on our backs
through time,
while above us
gulls convene in mobs
and awaken us with
the rude squabble of wings.

A Year Doing Nothing

includes walking downtown
to savor its skies and a cup of coffee.
A stop at the library to scan shelves
for poems by brothers in distress,
or a biography of a spy I'd once met
and who died in a room at
the end of the hall.
Or go right to my book in discards
and read feverishly... *Damn,
this guy ain't bad!*
Outside I'd light up,
lounge at the bus stop
and marvel at how
even the horizon
is lopsided.

Tao, a handbook

Once I'd read the ancients
like it were something
to be got through
as a dues-paying member
of the fraternity.
Now I hardly bother,
but when I do
it tends to soothe and
soften the edges
of days at the window.
When it's too much
energy to do something,
do nothing, says the text.
But be sure to leave
the handbook
where you found it.

Poems Like Us

I'm a long-term patient at
this place in the woods,
in the foothills of a range
thought ancillary
at the onset of bad weather.
I'm now at a stage in life
I've been stripped of honors
and issued a number.
I tend to leave the lights on
when I exit a room.
Everything is noted
in my file, but nothing changes.
I thought it's what I came for
but grew tired of asking
What was I thinking?
The nights are moonless, misty
and silent but for the ground
clearing its throat.
"Enough of the metaphors,
now brush your teeth!"
scolds the nurse who
doubles as a muse.
Or is it the voice in my brain?
You see, I'm a patient here
for confusing myself
with others.

Night Prayers

Both my children peeled off
as much as I've raised them to.
Now I find myself in the halls
of an asylum praying for my life
in the eyes of lunatics
whose words are bathed
in a noxious mist.
At night the dark comes
upon me like a lid.

Siren Call

Gazing at the bird's shadow
on the wall, I let my eyes
linger and sag,
and the ears sort out
the thousand appointments
made far away where
sirens flare on cue.
Help it get to where it's going,
and me, that I may
let go of these days
of waiting and
be by myself
whole and
awaited.

Out-of-Body

This old inebriate,
patient with what it takes
to get over his body,
lives in its shadow and
mops up the spillage.
Dropping his morning pills,
he crawls in the hall and wonders
where am I, why am I here?

The phone rings, it's a stranger
with urgent business that
needs transacted.
But he cannot bear
to listen and is it half
on purpose? We
cannot be sure.

Walt Whitman Takes the Greyhound

You'll spot him hunched over on a bench in a blizzard,
waiting out a 5-hour layover in Chicago
for a bus to New York.

He'd boarded in Bozeman, it seems weeks ago—
after reading his latest at the school there
to commemorate the fallen at Little Big Horn.
Attendance almost zero.

They chose to hide him when he stepped off the bus,
vomit-smeared, reeking of lozenges.

He didn't stay for the workshop,
or lessons in how to conduct oneself with a publisher.
They put him up at the Longhorn Hotel
and bought his ticket home.
You know how it goes.

Thank God the dean's wife stuck a twenty in his coat,
folded with the wrapped sandwiches.
Chicken salad, nibbled in back of the bus
across Dakota, Iowa, coming to Chicago.

Hence the 5-hour delay in the cold without whiskey,
or a place to take a piss.
The thought crossed his mind he might die
before a bus honked and the man bark
All Aboard!

They wouldn't know who he was till the snow melted.

Late Call

My friend gives herself
two years to live. Yes, two
sounds about right—
with an option to extend, of course.
The old world's finished.
We do what needs be done
to ease some way through it.
But wake us up with a word
or scrap of old song or
an apparition left over
from youth, you may
renew our contract with the living—
but hurry before we change our minds
or otherwise forget.

Travels with Charley

As a kid I'd bought it
on my own to read in my uncle's car.
Steinbeck, of course, and his poodle
taking off in a camper and
crossing New York State
into Pa. at a point where
my hometown lay.
In less than a sentence
he drives past it without stopping.
Critics were less than enthused
with his old whiskey charm.
The book lacked a profound need
to be written, they said,
thus failing to pack a punch
or a message worthy of a Nobel laureate.
But after a hundred pages
he pulls up somewhere in the Rockies
and meets the kind of drifter
I would aim to become
after many failed attempts
to take hold at home
and be someone.

The End

You'll not require diagnosis
to know it close up.
The space between you and me
plucked from the literature,
fixed and plaintive.

From this poem may you
salvage the words in Cyrillic font
from an unheralded dialect
of the steppes, its harsh
bunker slang, blunt
and without flourish,
the heart hunkered with
concrete nouns and
frozen fingers that
scratch for a bone
like barbed wire.

Back from the clinic,
may you discover a renewed
devotion to rapture—
deep, dreamless and
beyond all communication
with the living.

You will cobble this poem from nothing.

Vermeer

The woman at the table
wears an apron with pockets.
Ample, broad-shouldered, pale,
hair coming loose from its tie,
she waits…

Most women met in paintings
are real and appear
in daylight only after
being forgotten.

I write thin books nobody reads,
another guy pushing eighty,
who every time he shaves
swabs with toilet paper
and misses.

I've no idea why I'm here.

Sit down, she says,
and goes to fetch a towel.

Days Without Grace

Heat is hard on the old ones,
especially those who live alone
after losing a spouse and
their children long gone.
Due to financial hardship,
it's too late to move elsewhere
as fatigue and derangement
forbid it.

A tour is suggested as the price
of seeking comfort with others,
but only serves to make one
lonely in the end.
Back home you'll renew
your subscription to silence
and do everything in your power
to make sure things
remain the same.

Missing Person 46

When I am lifted up from the earth...
  (John 12:32)

After she dies you walk around
and talk to yourself like a
drunken tour guide.
Growing up, you will spy
on the backs of taverns
meant for deliveries
and watch men in aprons
pushing hand trucks,
then disappear at the end
of the alley.

You will trek a long course
without heart in the alley
behind things, and prefer
to wait to come forth
refreshed in the sky.
It's what was meant
from the beginning
and before that.

She's gone, so learn
the rules for passing through
to witness and report back.
It's all right, she soothes
smiling in the clouds,
you're doing fine.

Exerunt

At Hanging Gardens
friends are fixing to leave in clusters.
It came as a shock to get back
from the coast and see Bill
on my way to the mailbox.
He said he aimed to leave
for Michigan in a week
to see about an apartment.
I said it sounded like a man
feathering his nest,
and he shrugged and said
everybody's up 'n left,
Why not me?

Since last year's storm
when the trees fell on our roofs
and landlords hung us out
for the insurance—
(not to mention a power outage
and record temps by noon)
decay has set in.
Mold appears in corners
and cracks in the foundation.
Now going to the mailbox
a sad and lonely errand,
talking to friends about leaving
without saying goodbye.

Dear Diary

I am naked alone in my chair
in Pitch Fork, Arizona
[2014].

Or I'm naked on M's couch
while she tells me about
how things are and
how they must end
[2015].

I am naked on a bed
in a friend's spare room,
listening to men in the alley.
Vancouver [2016].

Or I am naked on a toilet
praying for strength of purpose
[2017].

Now I'm in a motel watching TV
to keep from going crazy
[2018],

or I'm naked alone on a cot
at my sister's house,
listening to wind off the Cape
[2019].

Next I'm upstairs
at a window overlooking the ocean...
[2020].

Dear God, I'm so tired
of running from being left,
there's no one left to leave me.

Getting Through It

What I want to know is
will it get me to the end?
I mean my car, my shack,
my teeth, my chair,
the last botched surgery
on my twisted hip.
        Just get me
to the end so I don't have
to mess with it when
desire's gone and
I burn my clothes
in the crapper and
toss my flip phone
in traffic before
veering onto a ramp.

At My Desk

a puddle of ketchup, coffee rings,
Sartre, Camus, Bergson, Mickey Spillane…
Modern times: the dragon flicks its tail,
one population scatters,
another rises.

An early sign of a culture
in free-fall is an obsession with
keeping score.

I'm sure someone noticed that
before I did.

2 Men the Same Age

(for Douglas)

Once we were old men sharing our latest
calamity with women.

Then we were just old men
forgetting our canes in restaurants.

Now we share a separation of silence
and sip our morning coffee.

Once we met, hugged, shook hands,
but could not see to see,

nor hear to hear. And now,
what is left for old men to say?

Laces

Bending down to tie my sneakers,
I cross one lace
with the other,
then pull.

Loop one lace around
your forefinger: hold,
wrap the other lace
and pull.

How many reps did it take
as a child to get it
and earn my mother's applause?
Look, I am weeping!

What He's Capable of

He'll leave a note to say
he's going for cigarettes
or the evening paper,
then goes and checks
into a deluxe hotel
and gets a room
high up and orders
a five-course dinner
with champagne,
then turns on the TV
and clicks through channels
for something mild.
*Yes, I do harbor
suicidal thoughts but
only during commercials.*

His wife reported
knowing something was up—
he doesn't even smoke—
but said nothing.

Later, he'll take a shower
and sit at the window
in a robe, watching the sky
turn color. He won't remember
swallowing the tablets
a few at a time. It's
quiet now, so peaceful
he feels it fill the room
and enter the hall.
He waits for it to fill

the glasses on his family's
table and open its arms
to the whole world in one
delirious hug.

At Reagan International

Coiled in a long, looping line
at Security, I spot them,
two Asian nuns, tiny,
bespectacled and
smiling like two
kittens in a blanket.
Perturbed by the wait,
I nod hello and they
squeeze with pleasure
to be recognized.
I prefer to think
their smile was just
discovered upon
finding me.
Yes, I was told
by angels at the kiosk,
always it was you,
or something like that.

Flight Manifest

After four hours aloft
and three hours adrift at
Dallas-Ft. Worth,
I've landed.
    No baggage claim,
I'm picked up out front
at Arrivals and driven home
by a friend.

Thank you for flying...

Home at last
alone with blinds drawn,
I wonder at my life
scattered among clouds,
while I collect their shadows.

Things to dispose of on earth:
cell phone, hearing aids, charger,
pills, my supplements…
my watch, passport, credit cards,
calendar, spectacles, underwear,
old shoes and books that
unravel, my bag, clock,
papers and every stick
of furniture.

Be sure to empty both
bank accounts and keep them
safe in an argyle sock…
jokes the old man who calls himself my friend.

Killing Time Between

Normally I'll not raise a big stink
about being out in public,

being of a tribe and place that can only
take the world in doses,

but I'd rather fry outside at 100 degrees
to drink their overpriced coffee

than be assaulted by the mayhem
raining from speakers in their ceiling.

Mother of God, I hope you find this
amusing, I hope you bust a gut.

You know I can't go on with this life
I've made up as I go along.

The Silence

The zither makes no music in its case.
　　　　—Deng Ming-Dao

Regarding this matter of taking up my trumpet…
pardon me, it can only come in steps
after collecting dust in a bottom drawer.
You might say I've lost my chops—
embouchure, the memory lips have
conforming to a mouthpiece.
Like recalling the kiss of a lost love
you have betrayed your taste for,
you're afraid to say hello and be
reminded of your failure,
your utter lack of character.
A man can only play if he's come
into his own. Hold it now, that's it.
Whether lifted to your lips or not
is not the point so much as
the life imagined after much pain,
a life of blowing the fire
from the ruins and
making it sweet.

The Famine

As a boy I longed to be alone,
patrolling sidewalks in scuffed shoes.
By adolescence and diagnosed,
I leaped from the car and fell
mooing in a bog of moo-cows,
then commenced to eat the grass.

My family goes back to the old sod
at the root. In dreams they comb
the softened earthen lumps
for bones, shards of kettle
where we're buried and
resume the terrible screams,
begging for food or to be
put down with the animals.
Skin-and-bone screams
to God in heaven.

Two hundred years on,
my father failed to warm to a new
family dog, nor his father his,
nor grandfather—when men stole
a neighbor's dog to eat
uncooked in darkness.
Let us appreciate then
the hunger that's brought us
to who we are. Let me sit
and write on an empty stomach,
and stare into my bowl.

Hummingbird Press

What, another poem?
How many does that make
just this year?

It's all I have, I said.
And besides, I've told you:
I don't write for prizes
but for the record.

By the fan's early whirring,
I float with the words
in my sleep, then
upon waking to
the smell of coffee,
I'll enter the light,
the faint tango of thunder
up from the Gulf.

At Rest

Some nights the black cat comes
to lounge on his haunches
in the shadows by
the quiet pool.

Neighbors know him enough
to stop and whisper
made up names
like he's someone they remember
wanting to know.

My Last Chance
for Andy V.

In the dream I work graves
at a motel I got fired from—
for pilfering, I think.
But that's another story.
Now I'm giving my report
to the day person who warms
to my coming on board.
A plain-spun woman
who walks with a cane
and remembers me enough
to look upon me sadly.
I don't recall a thing
that far back, so that take her word for it.
It's her hometown as well
as mine, and she knows where
to go for breakfast.
Besides, my friend Luke
who now owns the business,
says she's a good woman to know.
Listen, he says, *I mean it,
she would be good for you.*

You Will See the Ocean Before Dying

*...on earth nations in agony, bewildered
by the turmoil of the ocean and its waves...*
—Luke 21: 25-28

Close your eyes to see them,
the times and places
most longed for.

The Golden Gate at dusk,
her pearls blinking and
the bay sheer velvet.

Puget Sound at the end
of a floating life: islands, mountains,
the sun over China…

The Cascade pass
at Snoqualmie, the hush
of wind over immaculate snow.

Mount Hood bathed in gold,
crows gently mocking:
no one to call.

A Mojave bungalow
creaking in the first cool breeze
of the evening…

Weeping at last
for no good reason
but that there is a God.

The Last Reading

I made plain my desire
to read my latest,
but it hadn't arrived in time
to sign copies.
So I would read instead
from the manuscript
and hope not to trip
over corrections.
Not quite dark yet,
the evening lovely enough
to assign to memory—
friends on folding chairs,
my words rumbling off
like an apology for a life
made small by scribbling.
Afterwards they'd press
money into my hands
and thank me for nothing.

I Acknowledge…

So this is how it goes: fuzzy regrets, loss of purpose, excavation. Taking out the garbage. Measuring provisions to spread over each day. Making it last. Making it go longer…
Losing people—sudden, profound, carried off by the hour. A time to read the Russians. A time to turn off the phone and pray.

It's coming now, hear it, the thunder way off? It's the monsoon, and even if it's three drops long we count them to keep in a pouch. Yes my friend, our sweat is sweet—down deep and unseen. Sometimes it's only our absence that allows us to live.

I wish to thank those from the past year who laughed at my jokes and made me laugh and return to normal. Tom Burke as always, Ben Governale, to the people of Gotham Books, and my home in the high country. Best wishes to those who suffered my rants then got up to hug me. Jackie Goldman for one, Redama Hughes, Gary Belair, his wife Hong whose last haircut I still wear. To my daughters Cassie and Cornelia, and to Jane Anderson, her son Ryan and his family. To George Thomas and his wife Mertie. To Nancy on the Kenai, and to Andy Vinca and crew at Poets' Warehouse. To Louis, Rich, Chuck, Johnny O. and my cousin John P. who all keep watch on the lakefront. To Bear & Thasia, Mark B. & Janice, and to Mike and Barbara. To John Astudillo and his family in Ecuador. To Karen who sends me every quack remedy that works for her. And to all the others, so many and so few.

Already I can hear whole swaths of forgiveness slouch into place.

I forgive friends and kin for hurting me over stupid stuff. I forgive strangers their weirdness and for being in the way. I forgive why I left, and why I came back. I still have much to learn in forgiving myself—for nothing other than drowning in hell and subscribing to the daily down & dirty.

The Aztec poem that appears on the dedication page is from *The Daily Life of the Aztecs: On the Eve of the Spanish Conquest*, by Jacques Soustelle (1912-1990), translated from the French by Patrick O'Brien. New York: Macmillan, 1962. I stumbled upon it in Rebecca West's book *Survivors in Mexico*, edited by Bernard Schweizer, Yale University Press, 2004.

con abrazos y besos,
Tucson, 2024

About the Author:

Born in Erie, Pa, raised by good people and
taught to swim. French Creek, YMCA, the
lake when weather permitted. Raised free to
roam the docks, he found trouble that suited him.
He attended college off & on, and took satisfaction
in painting rooms with a roller. Following a stint
in New York, he drifted west, sobered, married,
had kids and moved inland. He fondly remembers
joining a cattle drive with his wife in Wyoming.
She was sensitive to horses.

www.ingramcontent.com/pod-product-compliance
Lightning Source LLC
LaVergne TN
LVHW041712060526
838201LV00043B/695